SCANDINAVIAN CROSS STITCH
on Linen and Cotton

Inga Bergfeldt

Stellar Publishing House / Search Press

Dedicated to my helpful friends, Greta and Brita.

Bergfeldt, Inga:

First published in the U.S.A. 1989 by Stellar Publishing House, Inc. 1304 Scott St. Petaluma, CA 94952.

First published in the UK 1989 by Search Press Limited, Wellwood , North Farm Road, Tunbridge Wells, Kent . TN2 3DR

Scandinavian Cross Stitch on Linen and Cotton (English translation by Lars Malmberg and Seymour Bress).

ISBN 0-9623468-0-2 Hardcover (U.S.A.)
ISBN 0-9623468-1-0 Paperback (U.S.A.)
ISBN 0-85532-658-1 (UK)

Typesetting and layout for the English Edition: Entropy Engineering

Title of the original Swedish edition:
Korsstygn i rutor och ränder by Inga Bergfeldt
Copyright © 1988 Inga Bergfeldt and ICA-förlaget AB, Vasteras
Graphics: Christer Petersson
Photos: Jan Tennek
Made and printed in Spain by A. G. Elkar, S. Coop.
Autonomía, 71 - 48012-Bilbao - Spain.

CONTENTS

Editor's Note

Materials Needed

This book was originally published in Sweden where linen fabrics and linen embroidery threads are readily available. Since those materials (8 thread per centimeter linen cloth, 16/2 linen yarn, and 35/2 lace linen yarn) are much more difficult to find in this country, we have modified the instructions slightly. In this edition, the instructions call for cork linen or 18 count cotton fabric and DMC or Anchor embroidery floss as well as the linen yarns specified in the original edition. If you use a smaller count fabric, your piece will be larger than the one illustrated; a higher count will result in a smaller piece.

If you wish to work with linen fabric and threads but cannot find them locally, you may obtain them from Glimakra Looms 'n Yarns, 1304 Scott St. Petaluma, CA 94952.

If readers in the UK and Commonwealth have difficulty in obtaining materials, please contact the British publishers, Search Press Limited, Wellwood, North Farm Road, Tunbridge Wells, Kent TN2 3DR.

American spellings have been used throughout this book; readers from the UK and Commonwealth please note that the equivalent word for pillow is cushion.

Finishing

In the projects which follow, most call for hemstitching, a type of decorative stitching. The diagram below shows how to stitch it.

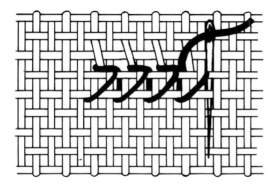

FOREWORD

This book is thought of as being a small handbook "for the times". That means that it is a book for you who, when evening comes, have done enough work for the day but still feel like doing something more - something relaxing. You who have worked with your brain the whole day might want to do something with your hands, something creative. You, who work with your hands might still wish to make something with your hands, but just for the fun of it. Why not sew something by hand, something rather easy in cross stitch, something that will have a fair chance of being completed within a reasonable time?

Many people like listening to the radio or to music, but still feel a sense of restlessness. Embroidering and listening to the radio or a favorite recording at the same time is no problem. It is also easy to combine watching the TV and doing needlework. Suddenly, to one's surprise, the work has grown several inches without too much effort, just from the pleasure of doing it. The pattern is not too complicated and it is pleasurable to see how the colors complement each other. The needlework feels nice in your hand, not too large, not too heavy and not too many stitches.

Cloth and yarn go together. Even the back looks tidy. (This was of great importance to the embroideresses of past generations!) After one or two weeks you have created something - a tablecloth or pillow for the home or for the children, a gift for a friend - an embroidery, subdued in color, which can be used anywhere and which will be enjoyed for many years, or an embroidery more "flamboyant" in color, which you really craved.

The embroidery, with its geometric patterns - squares, stripes and triangles, is worked in colors in harmony with each other - whether they are subdued or lively. These patterns and colors will not compete with others in your home, but will render an extra accent to it, as does a beautiful article of glass or ceramic. These small embroideries might free your creative powers during the work. The finished pieces might create happiness, a wish to try again and even a desire to create your own patterns. Anyway, that is my hope.

STRIPES

Fabric: Cork Linen (8 Threads per cm) or 18 Count Cotton

Yarn: Klippans 16/2 linen yarn or DMC or Anchor Cotton Floss

Size: 14 x 14 inches (30 x 30 cm)

Finished Size: About 9 x 9 inches (21 x 21 cm)

Charted Pattern: one square = 2 threads

	Klippans	DMC	Anchor
■	649	3012	854
/	658	Ecru	926
|	Half-bleached lace yarn or floss for hemstitching		

Start in the upper right hand corner by stitching the middle diagonal. Work diagonally downwards. Study the pattern carefully so that the darker stitches will be placed correctly!

GIFT FROM THE SEA

Fabric: Cork Linen (8 Threads per cm) or 18 Count Cotton

Yarn: Klippans 16/2 linen yarn or DMC or Anchor Cotton Floss

Size: 16 x 16 inches (35 x 35 cm)

Finished Size: About 12 x 12 inches (28 x 28 cm)

Charted Pattern: one square = 2 threads

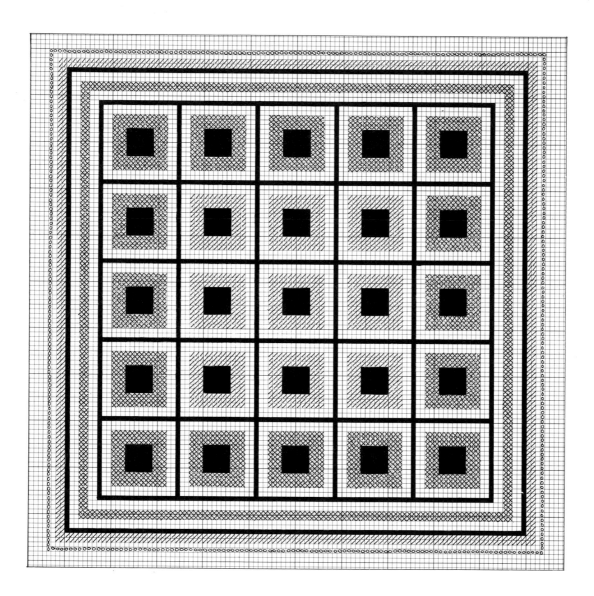

	Klippans	DMC	Anchor
■	523	524	858
×	610	842	376
/	658	Ecru	926
o	Half-bleached 35/2 lace yarn or floss for hemstitching.		

8

A Gift From The Sea, with its colors of the seashore, can be made into an attractive pillow. You can use it, for example, to give a subtle accent to an otherwise stark, white sofa. If you use it as a pillow top, leave about a 1/4" (5 mm) margin beyond the outermost margin of the design when you sew the backing to it.

LATE SUMMER SHORE

Fabric: Cork Linen (8 Threads per cm) or 18 Count Cotton
Yarn: Klippans linen yarn or DMC or Anchor Cotton Floss
Size: 14 x 14 inches (30 x 30 cm)
8 x 8 inches (18 x 18 cm)

Finished Size: About 10 x 10 inches (24 x 24 cm)
5 x 5 inches (12 x 12 cm)
Charted Pattern: one square = 2 threads
See page 63 for the pattern for the smaller version.

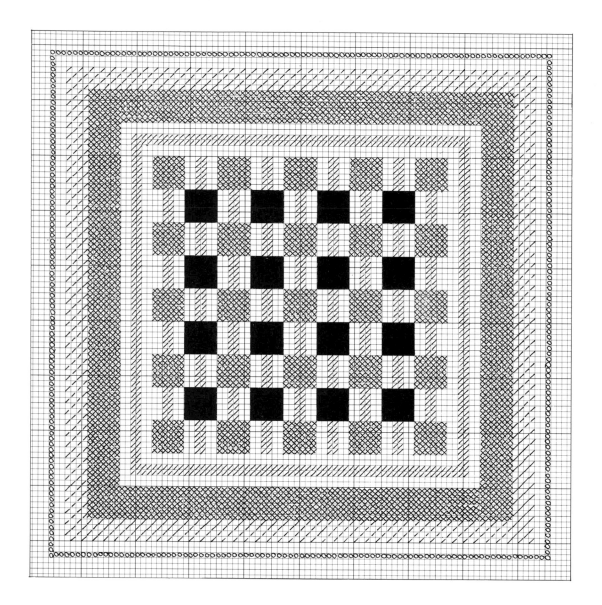

Klippans	DMC	Anchor
■ 571	762	234
× 509	3033	388
/ 600	white	2

o Half-bleached 35/2 lace yarn or floss for Hemstitching.

A late summer shore with light beige sand, well shaped stones - water polished, silver gray driftwood, ears of shore rye tormented by the wind, and the last white rose of summer inspired the colors.

QUEEN ANNE'S LACE

Fabric: Cork Linen (8 Threads per cm) or 18 Count Cotton

Yarn: Klippans linen yarn or DMC or Anchor Cotton Floss

Size: 18 x 18 inches (40 x 40 cm)

Finished Size: About 14 x 14 inches (34 x 34 cm)

Charted Pattern: one square = 2 threads

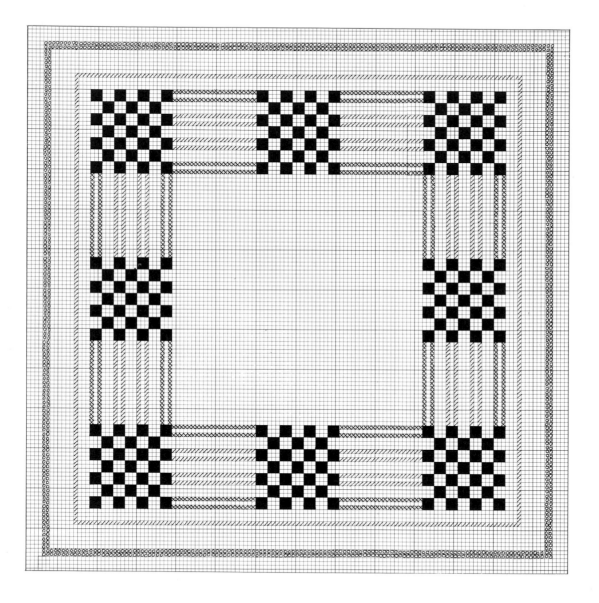

	BROWN PATTERN			DARK GRAY PATTERN			
	Klippans	**DMC**	**Anchor**	**Klippans**	**DMC**	**Anchor**	
■	514	640	832	516	318	400	
×	610	842	376	571	762	234	
/	600	white	2	600	white	2	
o	600	white	2	600	white	2	for hemstitching

The edging of the cloth, with its double row of hemstitches, worked in the same weight thread as is the rest of the embroidery, helps balance the brown and dark gray colors of the pattern.

SQUARES AND STRIPES

Fabric: Cork linen (8 Threads per cm) or 18 Count Cotton

Yarn: Klippans linen yarn or DMC or Anchor Cotton Floss

Size: 13 x 13 inches (30 x 30 cm)

Finished Size: About 10 x 10 inches (23 x 23 cm)

Charted Pattern: one square = 2 threads

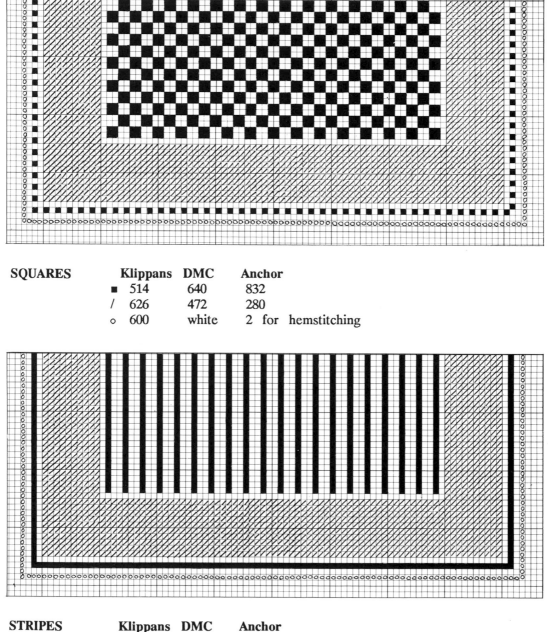

SQUARES	Klippans	DMC	Anchor	
■	514	640	832	
/	626	472	280	
o	600	white	2	for hemstitching

STRIPES	Klippans	DMC	Anchor	
■	514	640	832	
/	629	720	326	
o	600	white	2	for hemstitching

14

DIAGONALS

Fabric: Cork Linen (8 Threads per cm) or 18 Count Cotton

Yarn: Klippans linen yarn or DMC or Anchor Cotton Floss

Size: 13 x 13 inches (30 x 30 cm)

Finished Size: About 10 x 10 inches (23 x 23 cm)

Charted Pattern: one square = 2 threads

DIAGONALS

	Klippans	DMC	Anchor	
■	514	640	832	
/	583	322	977	
o	600	white	2	Hemstitching

Start the middle diagonal at the upper right and
stitch diagonally downwards.

A MASCULINE PATTERN

Fabric: Cork Linen (8 Threads per cm) or 18 Count Cotton

Yarn: Klippans linen yarn or DMC or Anchor Cotton Floss

Size: 17 x 17 inches (40 x 40 cm)

Finished Size: About 15 x 15 inches (34 x 34 cm)

Charted Pattern: one square = 2 threads

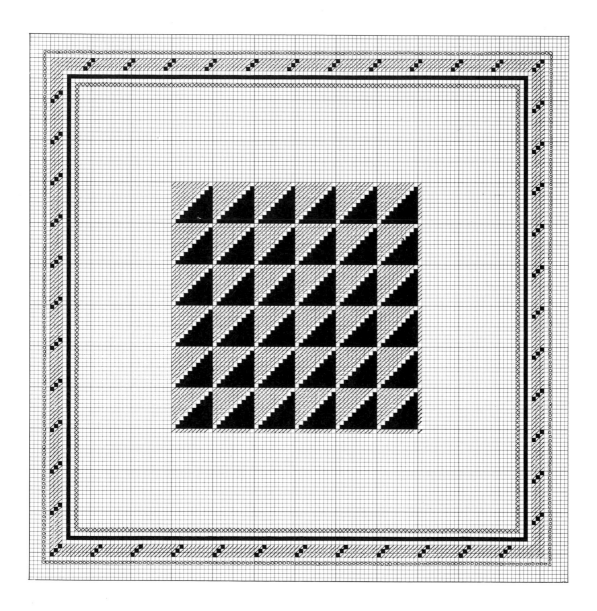

	Klippans	DMC	Anchor
■	648	317	236
×	540	321	46
/	523	524	858
o	Half-bleached 35/2 lace yarn or floss for Hemstitching.		

The central pattern gets a soft edging of light-gray at the bottom and to the right. Do not overlook it!

BASKETWEAVE

Fabric: Cork Linen (8 Threads per cm) or 18 Count Cotton

Yarn: Klippans linen yarn or DMC or Anchor Cotton Floss

Size: 19 x 23 inches (43 x 54 cm)

Finished Size: About 14 x 19 inches (33 x 44 cm)

Charted Pattern: one square = 2 threads

Detailed enlargement of the pattern on page 64

Finishing: Note that the hem is slightly wider at the left side of the mat (about 1/2 inch, 1 cm) and slightly narrower on the other three sides, (about 3/8 inch, 3/4 cm).

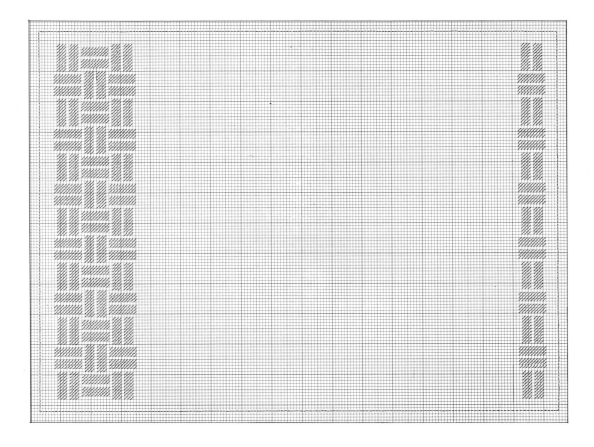

BEIGE TABLE MAT

	Klippans	DMC	Anchor
/	654	950	376

LILAC TABLE MAT

Klippans	DMC	Anchor
578	340	118

Table mats with interlacing embroidery like basketry, in lilac or lavender in July or in beige - like the grass by the roadside in August.

21

EARLY FALL

Fabric: Cork Linen (8 Threads per cm) or 18 Count Cotton

Yarn: Klippans linen yarn or DMC or Anchor Cotton Floss

Size: 18 x 24 inches (42 x 55 cm)

Finished Size: About 14 x 19 inches (32 x 45 cm)

Charted Pattern: one square = 2 threads
Detailed enlargement of the pattern on page 64.

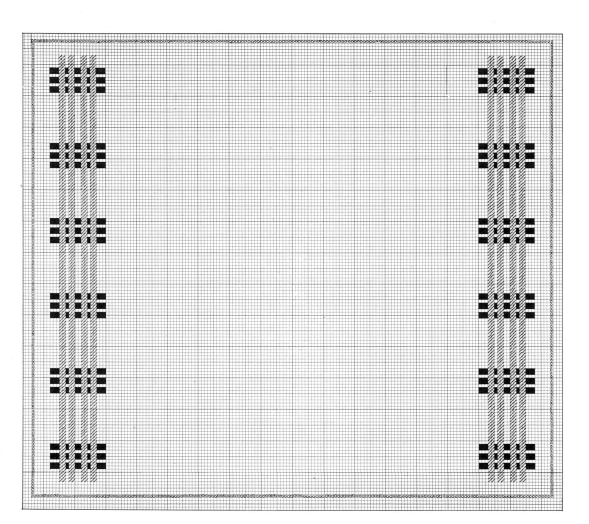

	Klippans	DMC	Anchor	
■	535	3705	11	
/	509	3033	388	
o	509	3033	388	Hemstitching

Even on weekdays it can be nice to set a beautiful table. Here is a table mat with an easy pattern in the colors of Autumn. Decorate it with a few rose hips when you lay it out.

PEASANT BLUE AND BERRY RED

Fabric: Cork Linen (8 Threads per cm) or 18 Count Cotton

Yarn: Klippans linen yarn or DMC or Anchor Cotton Floss

Size: 19 x 25 inches (44 x 58 cm)

Finished Size: About 15 x 21 inches (33 x 48 cm)

Charted Pattern: one square = 2 threads

Detailed enlargement of the pattern on page 64.

May be used as a place mat or as a small runner. The diagonals on the right and left sides are longer than those at the top and bottom. Study the charted pattern carefully so that the pattern will be correct at the corners.

	Klippans	DMC	Anchor
■	535	3705	11
×	663	958	187
/	585	964	185
|	Half-bleached 35/2 lace yarn or floss for hemstitching.		

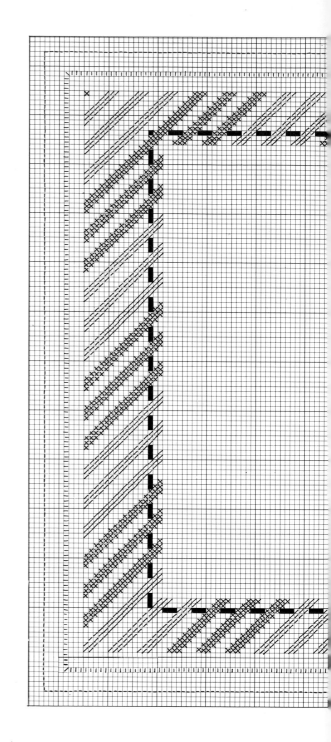

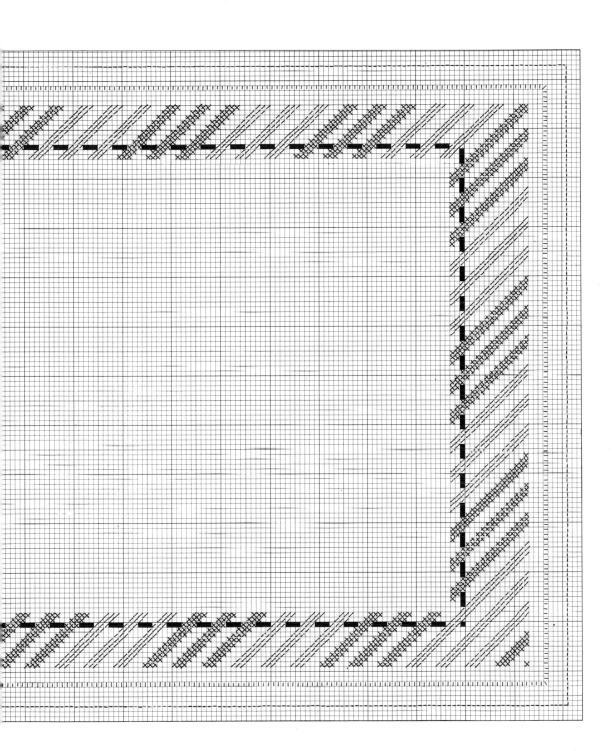

A FLOOR IN FLORENCE

Fabric: Cork Linen (8 Threads per cm) or 18 Count Cotton

Yarn: Klippans linen yarn or DMC or Anchor Cotton Floss

Finished Size: One repeat of the pattern, about 1 1/2 x 2 3/8 inches (3 x 6 cm)

Charted Pattern: one square = 2 threads

	Klippans	DMC	Anchor
■	516	318	400
×	514	640	832
/	571	762	234

A mosaic floor in Florence can certainly give inspiration to embroidery. This pattern is suitable for a chair seat, a pillow, a bag, or an eyeglass case, etc.

CITRUS

Fabric: Cork Linen (8 Threads per cm) or 18
Count Cotton
Yarn: Klippans linen yarn or DMC or
Anchor Cotton Floss
Size: 17 x 17 inches (40 x 40 cm)

Finished Size: About 12 x 12 inches (29 x 29 cm)
Charted Pattern: one square = 2 threads

	Klippans	DMC	Anchor	
■	595	970	330	
×	659	743	302	
/	598	445	288	
o	600	white	2	Hemstitching

28

Lemons, oranges and grapefruits have lent their colors to this cross-stitch embroidery. The cloth can easily be transformed into a pillow. Use a tight, thin linen fabric for the back. Leaving about a 3/8 inch (1 cm) margin around the row of hemstitches, sew the front to the back from the "right" side using small, fine stitches.

29

POT MARIGOLDS

Fabric: Cork Linen (8 Threads per cm) or 18 Count Cotton

Yarn: Klippans linen yarn or DMC or Anchor Cotton Floss

Size: 19 x 19 inches (43 x 43 cm)

Finished Size: About 14 x 14 inches (33 x 33 cm)

Charted Pattern: one square = 2 threads

Finishing: When hemming the finished piece, fold the fabric as thread- straight as possible. The width of the hem is 14 threads, and the fold should be made 3 threads from your last row of stitches.

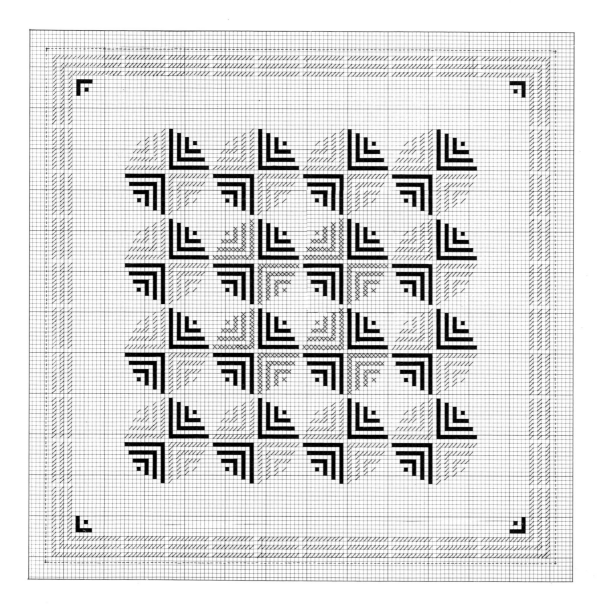

	Klippans	DMC	Anchor
■	595	970	330
×	596	741	314
/	659	743	302

An old Irish patchwork quilt was the inspiration for this embroidery which has borrowed its colors from the happy, sparkling Pot Marigolds. Use it as a tray-cloth.

SAND, SHELLS and CORAL

Fabric: Cork line or 18 Count Cotton
Yarn: Klippans linen yarn or DMC or
Anchor Cotton Floss
Size: 15 x 15 inches (35 x 35 cm)
Finished Size: About 11 x 11 inches (25 x25 cm)
Charted Pattern: one square = 2 threads

	Klippans	DMC	Anchor
■	535	3705	11
×	633	776	24
/	610	842	376
o	Half-bleached 35/2 lace yarn or floss for Hemstitching.		

You can stitch the middle part of the of this design easily and comfortably if you start at the upper right corner and work diagonally downwards - finishing each block of triangles of the same color before going on to the next color. Fewer color changes and a neater back!

33

FLAMING RED STRIPES

Fabric: Cork Linen (8 Threads per cm) or 18 Count Cotton

Yarn: Klippans linen yarn or DMC or Anchor Cotton Floss

Size: (front side) 15 x 15 inches (35 x 35 cm)

Finished Size: About 12 x 12 inches (25 x 25 cm)

Charted Pattern: one square = 2 threads

Assembly: Use a thin, closely woven fabric for the back of the pillow - the same color as the fabric you stitch on. Leaving a 1/2 inch (1 cm) margin around your pattern, sew the pillow together from the right side to get nicer corners. Stitches should be as small as possible.

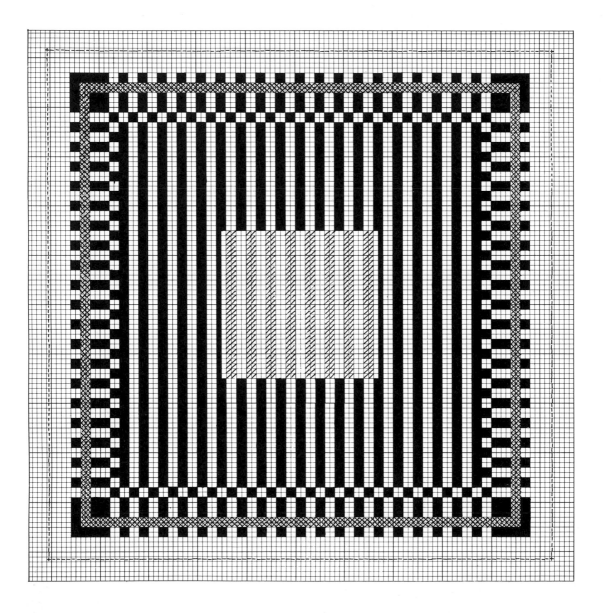

	Klippans	DMC	Anchor
■	540	321	46
×	573	957	54
/	595	970	330

Pillow with hot stripes and pillows of Thai-silk, 9 x 9 inches (22 x 22 cm) in matching colors.

34

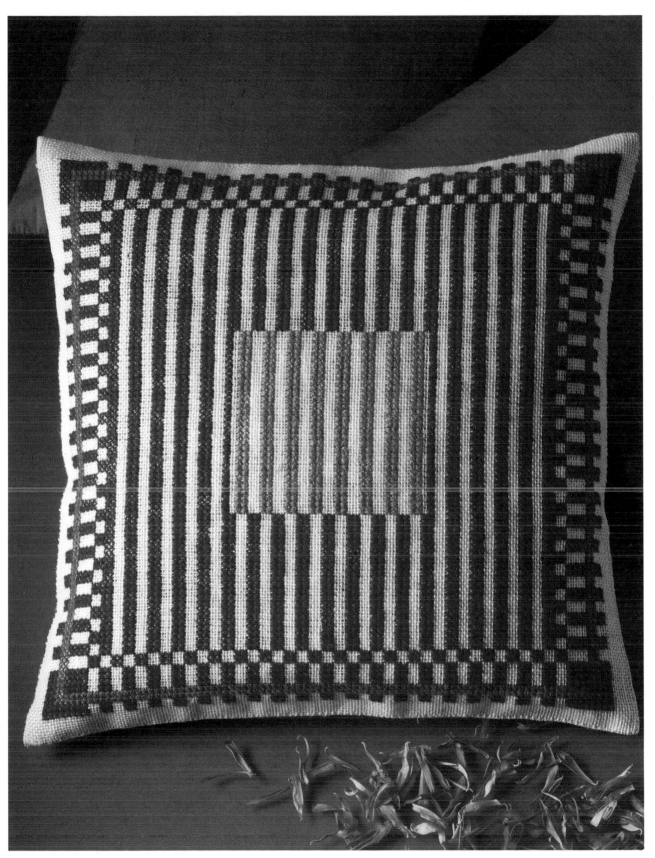

QUIET STRIPES

Fabric: Cork Linen (8 Threads per cm) or 18 Count Cotton

Yarn: Klippans linen yarn or DMC or Anchor Cotton Floss

Size: 15 x 15 inches (35 x 35 cm)

Finished Size: About 12 x 12 inches (27 x 27 cm)

Charted Pattern: one square = 2 threads

Finishing: Hem your cloth, leaving a 1/2 (1 cm) margin around your pattern. The width of your hem should also be 1/2 inch (1 cm). Make the hem with thread straight, razor-sharp folds. It does not matter whether you use mitered or straight corners.

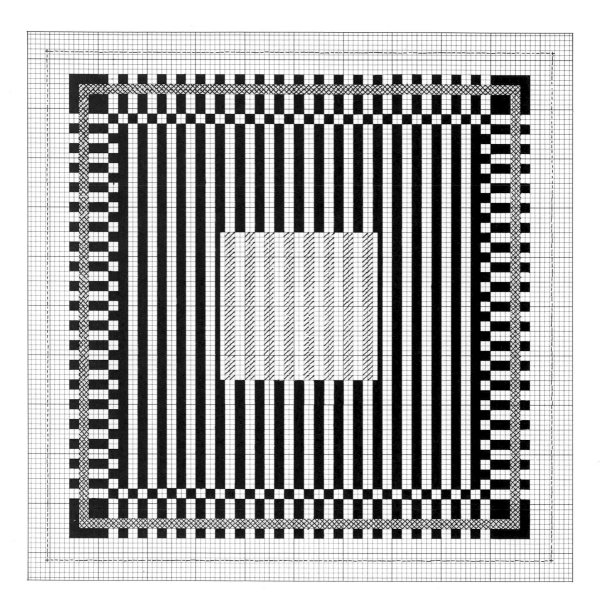

	Klippans	DMC	Anchor
■	514	640	832
×	602	932	921
/	585	964	185

SQUARES IN MOTION - Pillow

Fabric: Cork Linen (8 Threads per cm) or 18 Count Cotton

Yarn: Klippans linen yarn or DMC or Anchor Cotton Floss

Size: 16 x 16 inches (35 x 35 cm)

Finished Size: About 13 x 13 inches (29 x 29 cm)

Charted Pattern: one square = 2 threads

Assembly: Use a thin, closely woven fabric for the back of the pillow - the same color as the fabric you stitch on. Leaving a 1/2 inch (1 cm) margin around your pattern, sew the pillow together from the right side to get nicer corners. Stitches should be as small as possible.

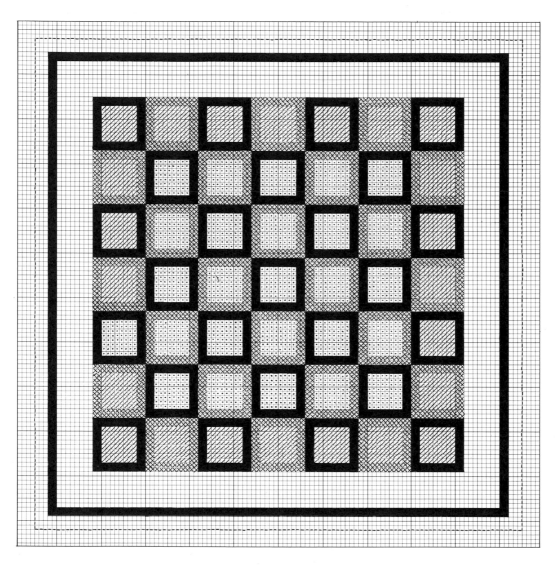

RED SQUARES			GREEN SQUARES		(See picture on front cover.)
Klippans	**DMC**	**Anchor**	**Klippans**	**DMC**	**Anchor**
■ 637	814	45	588	501	878
× 539	666	46	591	907	255
/ 620	353	8	518	563	207
● 633	776	24	517	564	206
			White	inside	border optional:
600	white	2	600	white	2

WHITE AND GREEN SQUARES - Pillow

Fabric: Cork Linen (8 Threads per cm) or 18 Count Cotton

Yarn: Klippans linen yarn or DMC or Anchor Cotton Floss

Size: 15 x 15 inches (35 x 35 cm)

Finished Size: About 13 x 13 inches (30 x 30 cm)

Charted Pattern: one square = 2 threads

Assembly: Use a thin, closely woven fabric for the back of the pillow - the same color as your background fabric. Leave a 1/4 inch (5 mm) margin around your pattern and sew the pillow together from the right side to get nicer corners. Stitches should be as small as possible.

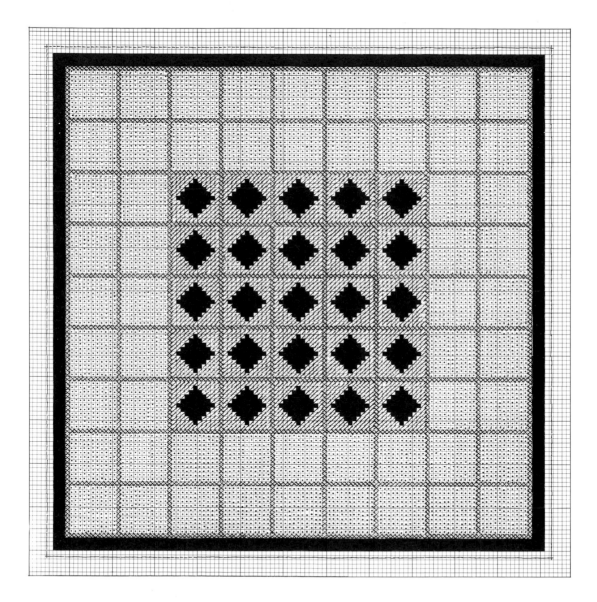

	Klippans	DMC	Anchor
■	628	937	845
×	589	470	267
/	653	772	253
•	600	white	2

40

WINDOWS

Fabric: Cork Linen (8 Threads per cm) or 18
Count Cotton
Yarn: Klippans linen yarn or DMC or
Anchor Cotton Floss
Size: 12 x 12 inches (28 x 28 cm)

Finished Size: About 9 x 9 inches (21 x 21 cm)
Charted Pattern: one square = 2 threads.

See page 62 for the pattern for the small
pillows.

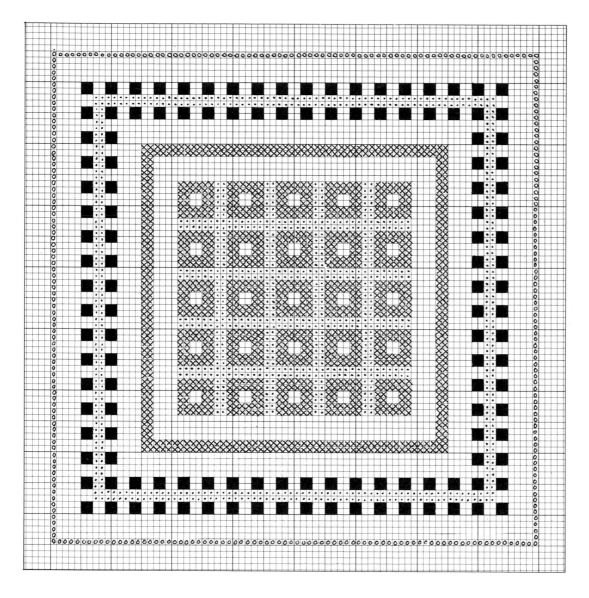

Coral			Blue Green		
Klippans	**DMC**	**Anchor**	**Klippans**	**DMC**	**Anchor**
■ 535	3705	11	663	958	187
× 633	776	24	585	964	185
● 658	ecru	926	600	white	2
○ Half bleached 35/2 lace yarn or floss for hemstitching.			Half bleached 35/2 lace yarn or floss for hemstitching.		

42

A LETTER IN THE MAIL

Fabric: Cork Linen (8 Threads per cm) or 18 Count Cotton
Yarn: Klippans linen yarn or DMC or Anchor Cotton Floss
Size: 12 x 12 inches (28 x 28 cm)
Finished Size: About 8 x 8 inches (18 x 18 cm)

Charted Pattern: one square = 2 threads
Finishing: Hem the cloth in the regular manner, leaving a 1/2 inch (1 cm) margin around your pattern. The width of your hem would should also be 1/2 inch (1 cm).

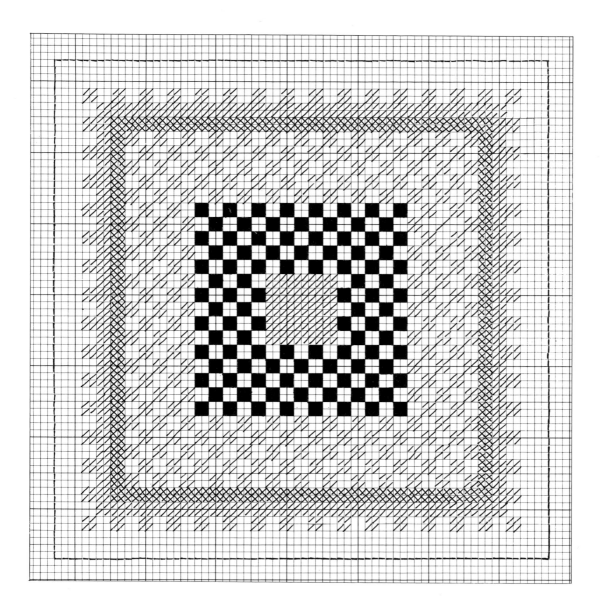

PINK			GREEN			BLUE		
Klippan	DMC	Anchor	Klippan	DMC	Anchor	Klippan	DMC	Anchor
■ 572	956	54	520	562	209	529	798	137
× 535	3705	11	591	907	255	583	322	977
/ 633	776	24	653	772	253	524	775	9159

44

Mail one of these cloths, wrapped in beautiful paper, as a gift to a friend - a little cloth in her favorite colors.

ROSES AND CORN FLOWERS

Fabric: Cork Linen (8 Threads per cm) 18
Count Cotton

Yarn: Klippans linen yarn or DMC or
Anchor Cotton Floss

Size: 11 x 11 inches (26 x 26 cm)
8 X 8 inches (17 x 17 cm)

Finished Size: About 9 x 9 inches (22 x 22 cm)
About 6 x 6 inches (13 x 13 cm)

Charted Pattern: one square = 2 threads

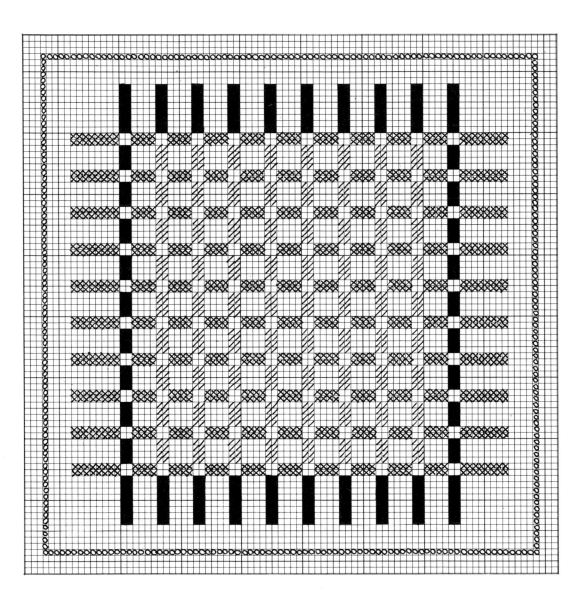

ROSES			CORN FLOWERS			
Klippans	**DMC**	**Anchor**	**Klippans**	**DMC**	**Anchor**	Use 3 strands of the
■ 625	3348	255	519	504	214	linen yarn or floss for your
× 576	3326	75	529	798	137	hemstitching
/ 623	605	50	583	322	977	
o 600	white	2	600	white	2	

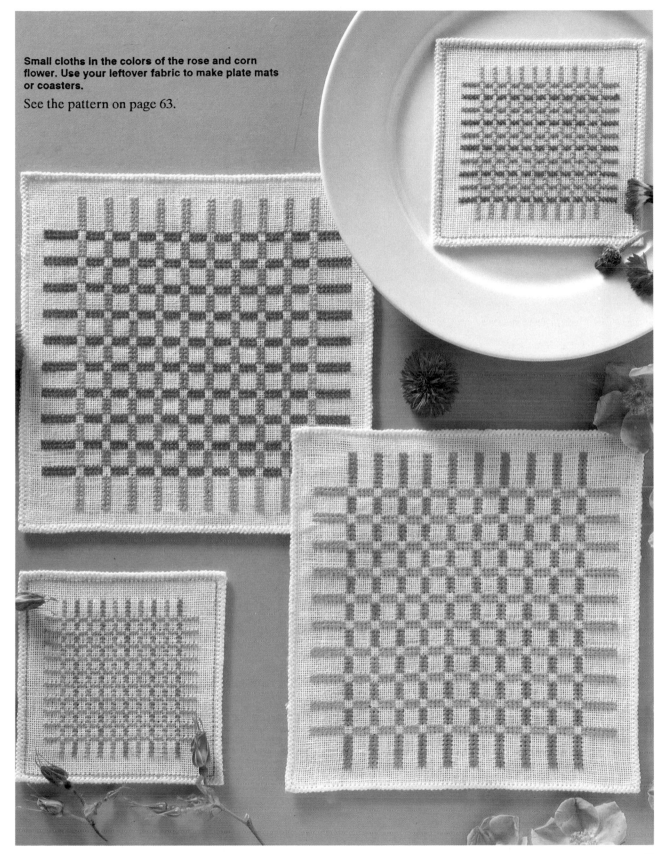

Small cloths in the colors of the rose and corn flower. Use your leftover fabric to make plate mats or coasters.

See the pattern on page 63.

47

A LITTLE PATCHWORK

Fabric: Cork Linen (8 Threads per cm) or 18
Count Cotton
Yarn: Klippans linen 16/2 or DMC or
anchor Cotton Floss
Size: 15 x 15 inches (35 x 35 cm)
Finished Size:
   Red: about 11 x 11 inches (26 x 26 cm)
   Blue: about 12 x 12 inches (27 x 27 cm)

Charted Pattern: one square = 2 threads
Finishing: Note: The Red cloth has a single
row of Hemstitching as a border around the
main pattern; the Blue cloth, calls for a double
row of those stitches.

RED PATCHWORK				BLUE PATCHWORK		
	Klippans	**DMC**	**Anchor**	**Klippans**	**DMC**	**Anchor**
■	539	666	46	529	798	137
×	576	3326	75	583	334	977
/	633	776	24	607	775	128
•	600	white	2	600	white	2
o	Half-bleached lace yarn 35/2			half-bleached lace yarn 35/2		
	or floss for hemstitching			or floss for hemstitching		

48

49

RUSTIC

Fabric: Cork Linen (8 Threads per cm) or 18
Count Cotton

Yarn: Klippans linen 16/2 or DMC or
Anchor Cotton Floss

Size: 19 x 19 inches (40 x 40 cm)

Finished Size: About 15 x 15 inches (31 x 31 cm)

Charted Pattern: one square = 2 threads

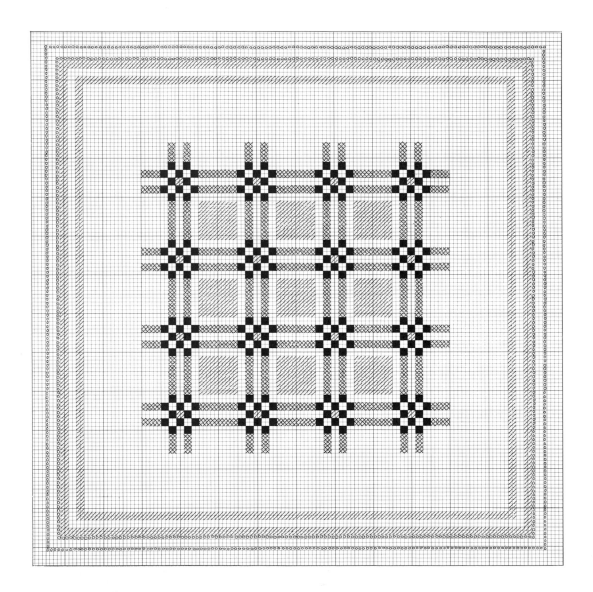

	Klippans	DMC	Anchor
■	539	666	46
×	573	957	54
/	623	605	50
o	Half-bleached lace yarn 35/2 or floss for hemstitching		

The pattern reminds us of an old handwoven coverlet, and the colors make us long for summer's geraniums.

THE GREENNESS OF EARLY SUMMER

Fabric: Cork Linen (8 Threads per cm) or 18
       Count Cotton

Yarn: Klippans linen 16/2 or DMC or Cotton
      Floss

Size: 17 x 17 inches (30 x 30 cm)

Finished Size: About 13 x 13 inches (24 x 24 cm)
Charted Pattern: one square = 2 threads

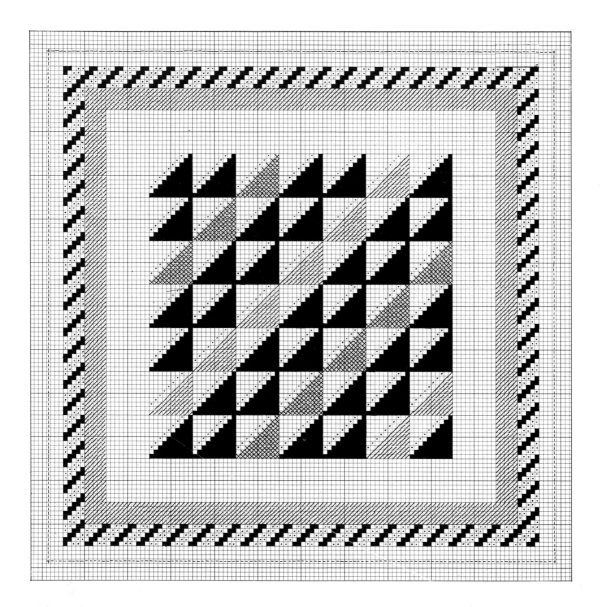

	Klippans	DMC	Anchor
■	625	3348	255
×	653	772	253
/	598	445	288
•	600	white	2

Cloth with rich embroidery in the yellow and greens of early summer. Start stitching at the upper right hand corner of the center pattern and work diagonally downwards.

SEDUM

Fabric: Cork Linen (8 Threads per cm) or 18 Count Cotton

Yarn: Klippans linen 16/2 or DMC or Anchor Cotton Floss

Size: 13 x 13 inches (30 x 30 cm)

Finished Size: About 11 x 11 inches (24 x 24 cm)

Charted Pattern: one square = 2 threads

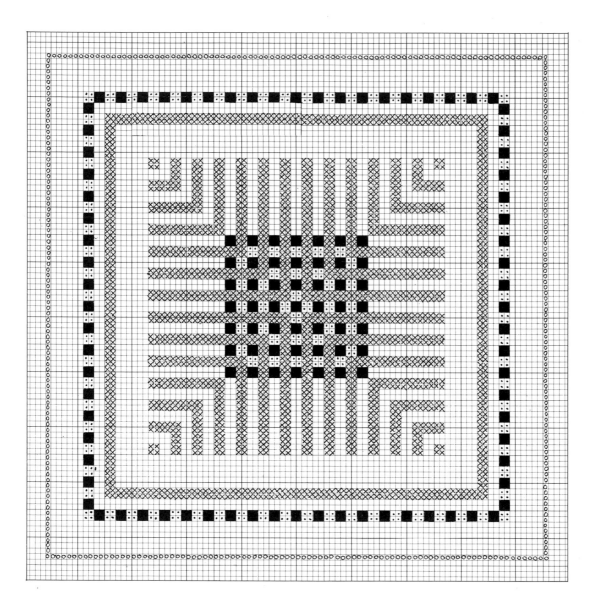

	Klippans	DMC	Anchor
■	628	937	845
×	653	772	253
●	600	white	2
○	Half-bleached 35/2 lace yarn or floss for hemstitching		

Small cloth and pincushion. For the pincushion pattern, see "Sachet Pillow 1" on page 60.

SWEET PEAS AND A LITTLE GREEN

Fabric: Cork Linen (8 Threads per cm) or 18
 Count Cotton
Yarn: Klippans linen 16/2 or DMC or
 Anchor Cotton Floss
Size: 13 x 13 inches (30 x 30 cm)

Finished Size: About 11 x 11 inches (24 x 24
 cm)
Charted Pattern: one square = 2 threads

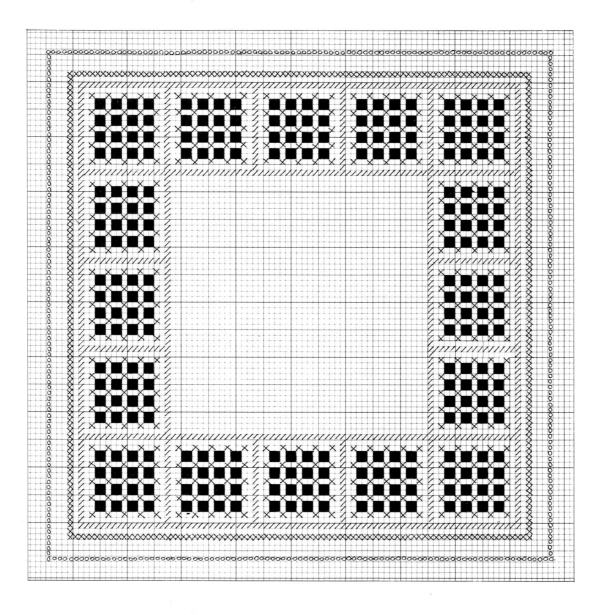

	Klippans	DMC	Anchor
■	520	562	209
×	518	563	207
/	579	3609	90
o	Half-bleached lace yarn 35/2 or floss for hemstitching		

LAVENDER

Fabric: Cork Linen (8 Threads per cm) or 18 Count Cotton

Yarn: Klippans linen 16/2 or DMC or Anchor Cotton Floss

Size: 7 x 7 inches (15 x 15 cm)

Finished Size:

Sachet Pillows: about 4.5 x 4.5, 4 x 4, 3.5 x 3.5 inches

11 x 11 cm, 10 x 10 cm, 9 x 9 cm

Pin Cushion : about 4.5 x 4.5 inches, (11 x 11 cm)

Charted Pattern: one square = 2 threads

Lilac Pin Cushion, (see the pattern for dried roses on page 60.)

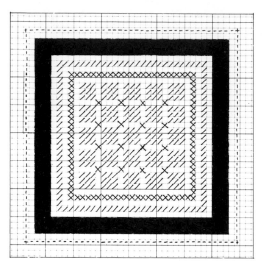

SACHET PILLOW 2

Klippans	DMC	Anchor
■ 664	522	262
× 642	552	112
/ 578	340	118

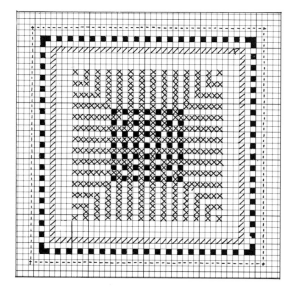

SACHET PILLOW 1

Klippans	DMC	Anchor
■ 643	550	102
× 609	341	117
/ 519	504	214

Assembly: When sewing the backing to the sachet pillows shown on this page, leave a margin of three threads from the pattern border. Use a fine, tightly woven half-bleached linen fabric for the backing. Sew from the front with small, fine stitches. Fill them with wadding and lavender. Assemble the pin cushion the same way as the sachet pillows.

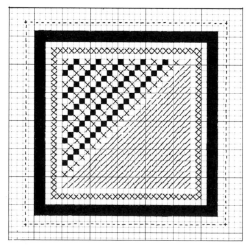

SACHET PILLOW 3

Klippans	DMC	Anchor
■ 643	550	102
× 664	522	262
/ 578	340	118

58

Fill the small pillows with lavender and wadding.
The wadding makes them elastic. The lavender
gives them a delightful fragrance.

59

DRIED ROSES

Fabric: Cork Linen (8 Threads per cm) or 18
count cotton
Yarn: Klippans linen 16/2 or DMC or
Anchor cotton floss
Size: 6 x 6 inches (15 x 15 cm)

Finished sizes:
Sachet pillows: about 3.5 x 3.5, 3.75 x 3.75, 4 x 4
inches
about 9 x 9 cm, 9.5 x 9.5 cm, 10.5 x 10.5 cm
Pin Cushions: about 4 x 4 inches (10.5 x 10.5
cm)

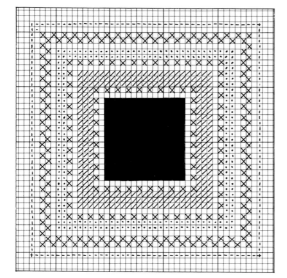

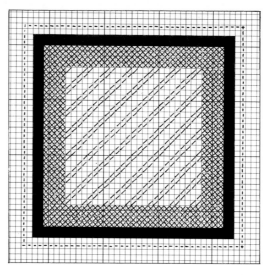

PIN CUSHION, beige

	Klippans	DMC	Anchor
■	654	950	376
×	532	818	23
/	509	3033	388
●	600	white	2

PIN CUSHION, lilac (See photo on page 59.)

	Klippans	DMC	Anchor
■	643	550	102
×	589	470	267
/	578	340	118
●	609	341	117

SACHET PILLOW 1, with edging in two shades of pink

	Klippans	DMC	Anchor
■	576	3326	75
×	532	818	23
/	658	ecru	926

SACHET PILLOW 1, with edging in two shades of green (See photo on page 55.)

	Klippans	DMC	Anchor
■	649	3012	854
×	532	818	23
/	658	ecru	658

**Fill the small pillows with leaves of old-fashioned
scented roses. Include a few spices like
cinnamon, cloves and mace. Also, use some
wadding to make the pillows a little more springy.**

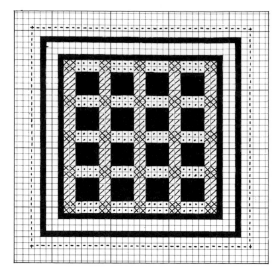

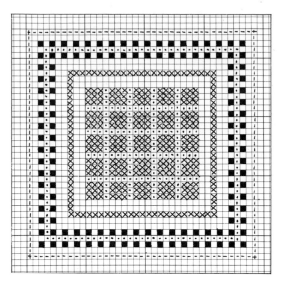

SACHET PILLOW 2, with thin pink edging
(See photo on page 61)

	Klippans	DMC	Anchor
■	576	3326	75
×	532	818	23
/	598	445	288
•	600	white	2

SACHET PILLOW 4, with coral pink edging
(See photo on page 43

	Klippans	DMC	Anchor
■	535	3705	11
×	633	776	24
•	600	white	2

SACHET PILLOW 4, with bluegreen edging
(see photo page 43)

	Klippans	DMC	Anchor
■	663	958	187
×	585	964	185
•	600	white	2

Assembly: Use a thin, closely woven fabric for the back of the pillow - the same color as your background fabric. Leave a 1/4 inch margin around your pattern and sew the pillow together from the right side to get nicer corners. Stitches should be as small as possible. Fill the pillows with wadding and dried, scented rose leaves.

The pincushion is made up the same way as the sachet pillows.

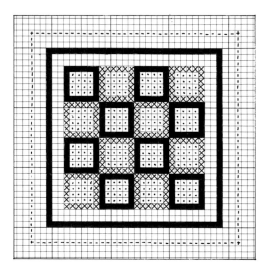

SACHET PILLOW 3, with hot pink edging
(See photo on page 39)

	Klippans	DMC	Anchor
■	572	956	54
×	535	3705	11
/	633	776	24

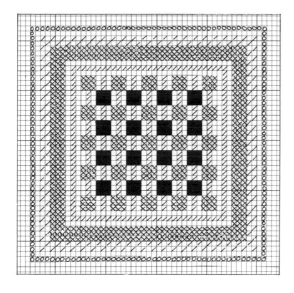

LATE SUMMER SHORE (photo page 11)

	Klippans	DMC	Anchor
■	571	762	234
×	509	3033	388
/	600	white	2
o	Half-bleached lace yarn 35/2 or floss for hemstitching		

MATS: The Rose and the Corn Flower (Photo page 47)

ROSE

	Klippans	DMC	Anchor
■	625	3348	255
×	576	3326	75
/	623	605	50
o	600	white	2 hemstitching

CORN FLOWER

	Klippans	DMC	Anchor
■	519	504	214
×	529	798	137
/	583	322	977
o	600	white	2 hemstitching

Note: The hemstitched strip can also be sewn 10 threads from the pattern and a green back-stitch stripe is sewn between the 8th and the 9th thread.

Detail, table mat: **Early Fall**　　Detail, table mat: **Basketweave**

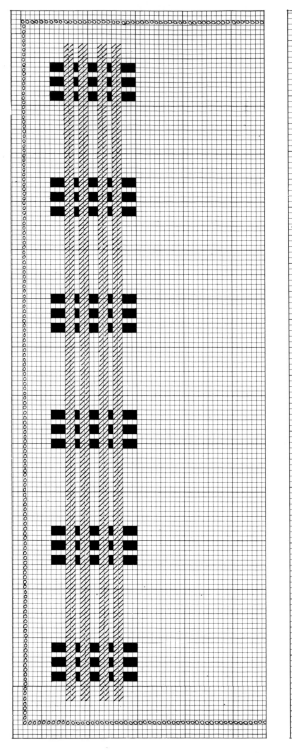